NARCISSISTS
101

Beginners guide to understanding and
dealing with a narcissist

Noor Niami

NARCISSIST 101

Copyright © 2020 by Noor Niami

Published by: Noor Niami

For information contact:

Noor Niami

www.noorniami.com

First Printing, 2020

ISBN: 978-0-6489327-4-1 (paperback)

DISCLAIMER:

THIS INFORMATION IS FOR EDUCATIONAL PURPOSES ONLY AND IS NOT INTENDED TO BE A SUBSTITUTE FOR CLINICAL CARE OR LEGAL ADVICE. PLEASE CONSULT A HEALTH CARE PROVIDER OR LEGAL PRACTITIONER FOR GUIDANCE SPECIFIC TO YOUR CASE.

"You can't create something real with someone fake."

Noor Niami

Dedicated to you

Don't wait for the light at the end of the tunnel, become the light you need instead.

This is my intention for you and for the world.

Acknowledgment

I have always wanted to write about this topic but I wasn't ready to write about something I was still going through. My pain was still raw at the time but I knew that one day, when I was ready, I would sit here and be writing on it from my personal experience. Fast forward to now and here you are holding the creation of a new book in your hands.

First and foremost, I would like to acknowledge my God and my Lord and Savior, Jesus Christ. My redemption, healing and restoration wouldn't have been possible if it wasn't for the love and mercy of God through Jesus Christ. God healed me back to wholeness and rebuilt me back up after being broken but this time round He built me up on the one true rock, Jesus Christ.

When the world rejected me, God accepted me. When the world broke me, God healed me. And when the world hated me, God loved me. God turned that little broken girl into a woman of truth, power, and wisdom. I am a living example that God turns broken things into beautiful things and He turned my brokenness into beauty and my pain into purpose. None of this would've been possible if it wasn't for His unfailing love, grace, and mercy so I give all the glory to God.

The Lord is my strength and my shield, my heart trusts in Him.

Secondly, I wouldn't have gotten through the darkest times of my life if it wasn't for my beautiful parents. They saw me at my absolute worst and darkest times. They helped me in ways I can't describe and I don't know where I'd be today if it wasn't for them.

And to my mum, Hana; I wouldn't be the woman I am today without your unconditional, unlimited love and kindness. You gave me strength when I was weak, you gave me hope when I was hopeless, and you gave me courage when I was afraid. You lifted me up every time I fell and you loved me even when I was hard to love. You never gave up on me and always believed in me even when I couldn't believe in myself. You helped me become the woman I am today and no matter what I do I'll never be able to repay you for everything you've done for me. You are my strength, my joy, and my blessing sent from above.

So to you mum and dad, I love you more than words can describe and I thank you for being by my side every step of the way. You are the light and the love of my heart.

Introduction

Narcissists 101 is a beginners guide to understanding and dealing with a narcissist. Dealing with a narcissist is anything but easy; it is confusing and daunting. Nothing about them makes any sense and the more you try and figure them out the more confused you become. How could someone who claims to love you hurt you this much and how could you love someone who is hurting you? Confusing and heartbreaking at the same time right?

So in this book I share insight from personal experience about what lies beneath the narcissist; revealing the basic characteristics of a narcissist and why they do what they do. This book shares with you basic, simple truth easy to understand and comprehend to help you make sense of all this nonsense.

There is so much more to be said and explained on narcissists and narcissistic abuse which I will later explain in my next book revealing a higher level of truth but for now, I wanted to keep it simple and basic to gently guide you into all truth.

No one will understand what you are going through or the heartbreaking, soul-crushing pain you endure from narcissistic abuse unless they have personally experienced it and lived it. But I am here to assure you that you are not alone in this experience because I and so many other people have been through it too.

And take it from someone who has been through it personally, there is a new life awaiting you on the other side of your healing. True love, genuine happiness and ever-lasting joy awaits you once you have healed and rebuild yourself back up into the person God has ordained you to be; and this is the other side of narcissistic abuse.

And when you actually think your life is over, this is when it has actually begun. And I promise you from the bottom of my heart, from someone who's been through what you're going through; the pain that you've been feeling now can't compare to the joy that is coming.

With love & light,

Table of Contents

"Narcissists try to destroy your life with lies because theirs can be destroyed with the truth."

- Unknown

Narcissists hide their true identity

Narcissists hide their true identity by putting on a false self; pretending to be someone they're not. They don't want to face the truth of who they are or their feelings of unworthiness and emptiness so they choose to be a fictitious character instead. But sooner or later this false self can't stand the test of time and the cracks will start to appear and you will start to see them for who they really are. You will start to discover they are not the people you thought they were and this is when you have to bring yourself to the stage of acceptance. Accepting this one powerful truth; who you thought this person is or who you wanted them to be; doesn't exist. And once you know the truth the truth shall set you free.

Narcissists love being the victim

Narcissists love playing the victim. They hurt you more times than you can remember but with every time they pretend to be the ones hurt. They act as though you have hurt them and will make you feel guilty for something they did. They make you feel sorry for them to avoid responsibility so you now have to work hard to please them instead. They distort the truth and tell a different version of the story; a version where they play victims. They do this for many reasons including not having to face the consequences of the things they did to you and also maintain a certain image to the public by showcasing that you're the one with the problem and you're the 'bad guy' in all this. Another reason why they love playing the victim is to gain all the sympathy and attention they can get from those around them and playing the victim will grant them just what they need. They always blame someone else for their own mistakes and never take accountability for their own actions because it's easier for them to believe there is something wrong with you than them.

The narcissist can't love you

It wasn't love that hurt you; it was loving the wrong person that hurt you. True love doesn't hurt, it heals; true love does not make you bitter, it makes you better. And if it didn't do any of these things to you then it wasn't true love. You can't find true love with someone who is fake; it is impossible because to feel and experience true love you need to be your true authentic self not someone fake trying to be real. So you can't have something real with someone fake. A narcissist is a false self; an entity that does not exist. Their character is all made up in their mind but the truth of who they are is completely different. They don't know what love is, they've never been exposed to true love or have the ability to generate that love from within. So they can't give you something they don't have because to give love you need to have love to give. They didn't love you just as you loved them and that's what hurt you; loving someone who didn't love you.

You can't find the truth in them

There is no truth to be found in a narcissist because everything about them is a lie. They lie effortlessly with no remorse because their whole life is based on one big lie. They are not real, they are false and everything about them is false so don't expect anything real to come from them. No truth can be found in a person whose whole character, persona and life are false; a fantasy that does not exist, a story based on a lie. They live in a fantasy they have created in their own mind so stop trying to find truth where it cannot be found. They have abandoned their true self and a false self cannot give you what only a true self can. Nothing can be real with someone who is false, always remember that when you're dealing with a narcissist. They come to destroy your life with lies because theirs can be destroyed with the truth. You and them are two opposing forces hence why the two of you could have never worked out. Narcissists lie to themselves in an attempt to run away from their truth, and if they lie to themselves then rest assured they'll lie to everyone else because it's easier for them to live a lie than face the truth.

They must put others down

They must put other people down to get a sense of superiority and greatness. They use their words to tear you down, criticize you and belittle you. That's the only way they can feel better about themselves; by tearing others down. They are jealous creatures, envious of anyone that could be better than them or have something they can't have. They start to diminish you by feeding your mind with lies that make you question your self-worth and value; they poison your soul with doubt and make you question your entire identity. They ensure that you don't see yourself for who you truly are so they put you down making you believe there is something wrong with you or you're just not good enough. They are critical and judgmental and the only way they can rise and have a sense of superiority and esteem is by putting others down.

You'll never be enough for them

You'll never be good enough for a narcissist because they believe they are God's gifts here on earth. They do no wrong and say no wrong; they are as perfect as it gets. They believe they are gods here on earth and as close to perfect as anyone could get so nothing you'll ever say or do will ever be good enough for them. After all you can't be as perfect as them. Can you see the delusion they live in? This is why you can turn yourself inside out and upside down and it still won't be enough. Nothing will ever be enough; they'll constantly be needing more and it is impossible for a human being to satisfy a narcissist. They'll always be asking for more, wanting more because they have an insatiable ego that will never be content or satisfied. The more you give the more you lose and they'll continue to take because that's the only way their false distorted self can survive. So don't take it personal; there is absolutely nothing wrong with you; no one and nothing will ever be good enough for them because this is the unrealistic fantasy they live in.

A child in an adult body

When you're dealing with a narcissist always remember that you're not dealing with a fully grown adult. Remember that you are dealing with an undeveloped five year old in an adult body. This is why you'll never get them to see sense because a five year old has no sense of understanding or logic. So don't expect a kid to act like an adult because that's just not going to happen. Narcissists haven't developed or matured like the rest of us due to childhood conditioning and they remain this way because they have no desire to grow or evolve. So when you're dealing with a narcissist remember that you are dealing with an undeveloped, immature kid and trying to get this kid act and behave like an adult is a mission impossible.

You can't reason with them

Don't waste your time trying to reason with a narcissist because trying to reason with a narcissist is like hitting your head against a brick wall. You won't get anywhere and you'll always feel like your chasing your tail around, going round and round in circles and never actually getting anywhere. It's mentally, physically and emotionally draining and you'll be damaging yourself in the process because a narcissist is anything but logical; they are illogical and nothing about them makes any sense. So stop trying to reason with them like you would with normal human beings because they're anything but normal. They will always find ways to disagree with you and make your life a living hell. They thrive on making people miserable so don't expect them to communicate with you as a normal person would. They believe they know it all and don't get it wrong and you can't reason with someone like that.

They have double standards

They have double standards; do as I say not as I do. All hell breaks loose if you do or say something wrong yet they get away with doing so much worse. And no matter how many times you try and confront them of their poor behaviour they will remain in denial and give you endless excuses for all the terrible things they did. They're good at making you feel guilty for something they did making it out to be your fault and they blame you for what they've done. They are two-faced with double standards; they want you to obey their commands and do as they say but don't you dare do as they do because they can't handle a taste of their own medicine.

They're quick to remember

They're quick to remember all the things they've done for you but will never remember all the things you've done for them. So nothing is ever genuine about them because even when they do something for you they're going to ensure it's for their own agenda and benefit. They will remind you of everything they've done for you even if what they've done was little to none. They use it against you to guilt trip you and make you feel bad for questioning them or pulling them up for their behaviour. Everything the narcissist will ever do for you rest assured that they will use it against you somehow, someday because everything ends up being about them some way or another.

Discarding their victims

When the narcissists have completely worn their victims out that's when they begin to discard them and move on to their next source of supply. The narcissist cannot survive without their supply so when they can no longer get anything from you that's when they usually discard you. Although this is excruciatingly painful it is nothing personal because the narcissist will do this to everyone they're with. It has nothing to do with you or your self-worth but everything to do with them and how they feel about themselves. They use people up then move on to something new when their resources are dried up. This is the final stage of a narcissist unless of course it was you who built up the courage to walk away from them. Narcissists will do this to everybody this is why they can never sustain a long-lasting relationship with anyone because they don't see people as people; they see them as mere objects to use for their own satisfaction and gratification.

They objectify people

People are not people to the narcissists; they are mere objects for their use and control. They dehumanize people and treat them as objects to use for the purpose of meeting their own needs. The narcissists' main concern is what they can get from you at any given moment and they will do what it takes to get what they need. Narcissists are not like normal people and they lack morals and human decency so they cannot function as normal people let alone see you as a person, with a heart and soul. They ignore your emotions, needs and concerns because they are incapable of having a heartfelt, genuine interaction with you or anyone else. But they can however see you and deal with you as an object for them to use for their own personal gain and gratification and they don't have to care or justify their abusive behaviour to mere objects.

They can't stand seeing you happy

Narcissist can't stand seeing you happy because you being happy sheds a bright light on their misery and reminds them of the fact that they can't be happy. They cannot experience true joy and genuine happiness because these are authentic feelings that must be generated from your true self. Narcissists have replaced their true self with a false one so they cannot experience anything genuine including happiness. They have to make believe and fabricate their entire life including their feelings. Hence the reason why they can't see you happy and they'll feel worse when your happiness has nothing to do with them and you're happy because of someone else or something else. They will attempt to ruin that for you one way or another because they cannot stand seeing you have something they can't have.

They make you feel lonely

Sometimes we choose to settle for way less than what we deserve because we don't want to be lonely. But being with a narcissist will make you know loneliness like you've never known before. You're with them yet they make you feel like you don't exist. You're with them yet they make you question your self-worth and value. You're with them physically yet so distant and alone spiritually, mentally and emotionally. Being with someone who makes you feel like you don't exist or matter is far worse than being on your own. Being with a narcissist will make you feel lonelier than you've ever felt before. You're with someone who doesn't see you let alone value you because the narcissists can only see themselves. Yet many people have chosen to settle out of fear of being alone but there's a difference between being alone and lonely. I don't know about you but I would rather be happy alone than be miserable with someone.

Your needs won't be fulfilled

Your needs will never be fulfilled with a narcissist, on the contrary, the narcissist will have you be in a state of constant neediness. The narcissists don't care about what you need or desire because your feelings to them are irrelevant. A relationship with a narcissist isn't a normal relationship because they don't see you as their partner but more of an admirer, an obedient worshipper. They see you as someone who is there to fulfil their needs by constantly telling them how great and amazing they are. You are an object of gratification to their insatiable ego, someone who is there to constantly validate their existence because without your attention they don't exist. This is why being with a narcissist will drain you; they will only empty you and never pour into you.

Narcissists don't want you seeing your worth

They will make you feel worthless and question your worthiness of being loved because they don't want you being aware of your self-worth and value. Deep within they know that you are worthy of more and deserve better than them and will attempt to keep this in the dark lest you find out the truth and leave them. Narcissists don't live in reality, they live in an illusion; a fantasy that doesn't exist and this includes the way they see people. They will make you see yourself through their distorted eyes but don't buy into that, don't believe the narcissist's version of who you are. They will do what it takes to undermine your self-esteem and worthiness because they want you feeling the same way they feel about themselves; unworthy, unloved, unappreciated.

It's never their problem

In the narcissist's world it will always be your problem or someone else's but definitely not them. They refuse to acknowledge their shortcomings and mistakes to protect themselves from the truth and bury feelings of inferiority and shame. So they project their faults on you by blaming you for something you didn't do. A narcissist will dump their distorted selves, issues and problems on you. Then they'll make you believe you're the one with the problem and there is something wrong with you. They will make you believe you're a bad person and characterize you with the same negative traits they possess. They will treat you as their punching bag and dump all their demons on you. But none of this is your fault because this isn't really about you. It's more about the narcissist running away from their tormented self by putting the blame on someone else; believing it's someone else's problem and not theirs. This is how they run away from their reality by shifting the blame on someone else and never taking accountability for their actions.

Narcissists use repetition

Narcissists use repetition to instill and engrave false beliefs in your mind. The use of repeated words or phrases will plant seeds of doubts in your mind and with time you begin to believe in these doubts making them your truth. So slowly you start to believe in everything the narcissist is saying about you, you start to see yourself the way they see you and you also start to behave like them in some ways. You will no longer recognise the person you are because you've become a reflection of who they are and this is when you forget the person you used to be. They use repetition of remarks, such as, 'you're overreacting', 'you're just over thinking it', 'why are you behaving like this', 'what's wrong with you', 'why can't you just be normal' and the list goes on. They will make these phrases subtly but you will notice them repeat the same statements over time creating self-doubt and confusion.

They need constant admiration and recognition

Being with a narcissist is draining because they need constant praise and admiration to keep their ego inflated. They are unlike normal people where the occasional compliment is sufficient; the occasional praise and admiration is not enough for the narcissist. They need constant attention because attention is food for their ego and without it the ego cannot survive. This is why you walk out of a narcissistic relationship feeling like twice your age; worn out, depleted and diminished because it was impossible for you to keep a steady stream of praise, compliment and admiration. They take and take from you but will give you absolutely nothing in return because a relationship with a narcissist is very one sided. It's about what you can do for them and what you can give them and not the other way round.

Being broken and being evil

There's a difference between being broken and being evil, don't confuse the two. A broken person doesn't go around hurting people on purpose and they can still show remorse and compassion. But an evil person causes pain deliberately and shows no compassion because the only person they care about is themselves. We can all have narcissistic traits because we all have an ego but what sets us apart from true narcissists is that we have a conscience that tells us this is right or wrong. Narcissists on the other hand don't; they don't care about what's right or wrong. All they care about is getting what they need at any expense even if it means destroying another person's soul. You may be broken but you still have morals, ethics and conscience; narcissists don't. So my point to you is you may be broken but you're not evil. A narcissist on the other hand is broken as well as evil.

They move on very quick

Narcissists move on quickly and I mean very quickly. This is excruciatingly painful to witness because while you seem to be drowning in your pain they seem to move on with their life as if nothing happened. But there's a reason why they do this and it has absolutely nothing to do with you. Here's why they move on so quickly; narcissists cannot survive without supply. Supply is someone else's attention and focus on them to validate their existence and experience because without it the false-self doesn't exist and they will be faced with their biggest fear and dread; being their true tormented self. This is something they will continue running away from all their lives and will do what it takes to keep that false-self propped up. So they need to quickly move on to their next source of supply because they cannot survive without someone else's soul. It has nothing to do with you or your worthiness of being loved, not at all. This has everything to do with them running away from their true-self by keeping their false-self fed and alive by having someone else's attention fixated solely on them.

They'll never choose you

Despite the utter confusion and the immense amount of pain you go through when being with a narcissist; you just have to make the decision to walk away and never look back. It's easier said than done I know that very well but there comes a time where you have to choose between them or yourself because the narcissist will never choose you over them. You will hold on to them at the hope that they too will hold on to you but to your disappointment the narcissist will only ever hold on to their false-selves. You will realize that they will never choose you or fight for you as you have done for them because it's easier for them to give up than to actually fight and put in effort. So you need to make a conscious decision, no matter how much it hurts, to let them go and choose yourself because you are far more worthy of the love you're trying to give them.

Enmeshed with the narcissist

Being with a narcissist will have you feeling like an addict because you are in essence addicted to them. What it means to be addicted to them is when you can't stop thinking about them, missing them, wanting them even when you know they're no good to you. They are the centre of your universe and you can't seem to focus on anything else but them. And by this time it would be impossible for you to envision life without them and even when you do leave the narcissist it would still feel like they are living inside of you. This is because you have been enmeshed with the narcissist and the two of you have become one. You no longer recognise yourself without them and this is why walking away from the narcissist is hard because you will leave a big part of you behind; a part you will never get back.

You don't have to explain it

You can't explain to anyone who a narcissist is or what narcissistic abuse is unless they have been through it themselves. You cannot describe it because to understand it you need to go through it. It is beyond our logical mind and the more you try and explain it to people the more they'll think you're going crazy. People will diminish your pain and undermine your situation because they don't know what you're going through. They don't know that you've just lost yourself completely and now you have to start again in building a new you and a new life. They don't understand that nothing remains the same and you will never be the same after the abuse. They're not living in your shoes, feeling your pain or fighting the battle you're fighting so don't try and explain or justify what you're going through. This is your pain, your story, your life and no one has the right to invalidate your feelings because they are real.

You can never fill them

How long have you and I spent trying to fill them up at our own expense? We emptied ourselves out in the attempt of filling them and fulfilling them yet despite all our efforts nothing was ever enough. That's because it is impossible to fill them up no matter what you do. Try and see the narcissist as a bucket with a hole; no matter how much you put in it, you'll never fill it up. The narcissists are exactly like that; they have a huge hole and nothing you give will ever be enough and all your hard work and effort will go down the drain. It is impossible to fill and satisfy their insatiable ego because it'll always want more and demand for more. But in the end you'll never be enough for the narcissist because no one and nothing ever is.

They are selfish

Narcissists are selfish, self-conceited and self-deceived people. They are full of pride and ego and they think everything evolves around them. They're good at emptying people out of their resources so they can become full of themselves. That's why narcissists leave you feeling empty and depleted because they have taken just about everything from your soul and when you have nothing else to give that's when they discard you and move on to the next best thing. Until they use up their next source and move on to the next. It's always going to be the same repeated cycle with the narcissists, from one soul to the other. But don't be discouraged because people like them can never find true love and happiness with one person. They're doomed and they're a curse upon themselves. Imagine waking up every day with the inner torment and the constant, never-ending pursuit of having to go out into the world for constant energy and supply in order to barely make it through the day and survive. What a life.

They treat strangers better than they treat you

They treat strangers better than they treat their own people. Have you ever wondered why they treat someone they barely know so much better than they're treating you? The person who is bending over backwards to fulfil and satisfy all their needs? How can they be so loving and kind to people they barely know yet so evil and malicious to those they know? And when you confront them about it they make believe you have issues, you're insecure, jealous and crazy. They make you feel horrible for something they're doing wrong and this is how they manipulate and abuse you. They also do this because they have an image to maintain in public. They need the world to view them as this incredible person who is thoughtful, loving and kind. This is the mask they need to wear to cover up who they really are on the inside; selfish, insecure and jealous people.

They'll never admit fault

The narcissist is unlikely to admit a mistake or be at fault. They will not take responsibility for their own actions or the pain they caused you but instead they project their behaviour onto you or someone else; always making it someone else's fault for behaving this way. Arguing with narcissist about this is futile because they will never admit they are wrong and they will continue lying and twisting the story over and over again until it's now somehow turned back on you and you're the one in the wrong. Haven't you ever wondered why on earth you were the one apologizing at the end of that conversation? They gaslight you and make you believe in their lies and you end up believing their version of the story thus being the one apologizing for something you didn't do wrong. They believe they are invincible and perfect so it'll always be someone else's fault and never at all theirs.

They can't have long-lasting relationships

They will get rid of people who no longer serve them or encourage their behaviour. They are incapable of having long lasting relationships or friendships. You'll always see them move from one person to another because they're not capable of nurturing and building a solid, genuine connection. They can only maintain a connection with people who have very low self-esteem because not everyone will accept their rotten unacceptable behaviour and keep quiet about it. They are not after genuine connection with real people; they are after admirers and supporters who will keep condoning their behaviour and validating their existence.

Narcissists only come to kill, steal, and destroy

You'll waste your whole life if you're going to wait for them to change or learn how to love you the way you want to be loved. Think of narcissists as thieves; they only come to kill, steal and destroy. They will kill your joy, steal your peace and destroy your sanity. They steal away your time by making promises they know they won't keep. They will say or do what it takes to keep you hooked in as their supply. The narcissist, unlike you, doesn't have a soul so they come after your soul and steal away everything that you are. They attempt to steal facets of your personality and your good characteristics, the things they don't and can't have. This is why you barely recognise yourself when you walk out of a narcissistic relationship because it seems as though they have stolen your entire identity and you no longer remember who you are. When dealing with a narcissist remember that they only come to kill, steal and destroy.

They will never compromise

Good luck trying to get a narcissist to compromise because there is no compromising with a narcissist. They believe they are right about everything and will not give you the opportunity to even discuss anything as two mature adults would. It's their way or the high way and if you disagree with them then they lash out as a little kid would. They won't compromise but expect you to compromise on everything and they will refuse to hear what you have to say or understand your point of view. They point blank don't care about what you think or how you feel and they are unwilling to meet you half way. They believe it's your responsibility to meet them where they are and give in to their way. They believe they are always right about everything so they'll never compromise and meet you half way. It's basically their way or no way at all.

They are extremely charming – at first

Narcissists are extremely charming and persuasive, at first. It all starts as the perfect fairy tale when they can't seem to get enough of you. When they tell you how much they love you and cannot see themselves without you. They say all the right things at the right time, they're either constantly texting you or wanting to see you and while this is all great, unfortunately it's not real. This is called 'love bombing', a form of manipulation and tactic the narcissist uses to lure you in. They 'bomb' you with extra amount of attention, affection, compliments, gifts; you name it, in order to get you hooked in and get your attention so they can begin to control you. Yes we all love to be seen and appreciated but real love takes time to nurture and grow whereas the narcissist will tell you they love you within the first month. They will do and say all the right things making them extremely charming and hard to resist but sooner or later you will realise this isn't who they really are and the mask will eventually fall off.

Narcissists are blame shifters

Narcissists will refuse to take the blame for anything even for the obvious horrendous things they've done. They will not take the blame and admit what they did was wrong and even when they do it'll be your fault somehow, always shifting the blame back on you. They will always shift the blame and put it back on you. You could be having a conversation with them about something you busted them doing or lying to you about something and somehow they'll make it be your fault. You will find that at the end of that conversation it'll be you who's sitting there defending yourself about everything you've ever done wrong in your life and all of the sudden the tables have turned and the blame's on you. Your feelings, your pain, your concerns are invalidated and ignored and you'll walk away wondering what just happened because you're back at square one. That's what narcissists do, they are blame shifters; shifting the attention off what they did wrong and putting it back on all your shortcomings instead.

Narcissists 101

They don't like to be alone

Narcissists don't like and cannot be alone because being alone would starve them to death; spiritually, emotionally and mentally. They don't like to be alone because it would mean being alone with themselves; the self they're trying so desperately to run away from and avoid. It would mean sitting alone with their demons and tormented self and that's one thing you'll never get the narcissist to do. This is why you find narcissists move on a lot quicker than most people because they don't sit there and give themselves time to process their pain. They are constantly running away from their pain therefore will never truly heal. Instead they go out finding another source of supply; someone who will give them the attention and energy they need to give them temporary relief from their pain. But the pain will always be there and the need to use people will always be there too. Nothing is more important to a narcissist than their narcissistic supply to soothe themselves from their inner torment and turmoil.

They will abuse your forgiveness

Narcissists cannot perceive or see things the way you do because unlike you, they're not real. They're a false character and cannot understand or appreciate anything of value. Forgiveness is valuable because it is an act of kindness and grace yet the narcissists don't see it this way. They abuse your forgiveness and use it as another opportunity to gain what they need at your own personal expense. The more chances you give the less they take you seriously. They begin to ignore your boundaries, continue to disrespect you and violate your truth because they know another chance will always be given. They get comfortable with hurting you and get away with their spiteful behaviour because they know they will be forgiven and another chance will always be given. They can't appreciate anything of value instead they will abuse your kindness for their personal gain. Whatever you do, don't let your forgiveness turn you into slavery. Forgiving them doesn't mean you give them another chance to hurt you with.

They will attempt to hoover you back in

The minute you start to feel okay, like you're finally getting a grip on your life after you've separated yourself from the narcissist it'll be the minute they reappear back into your life again. They will attempt to come back to your life more than once and will tell you all the things you want to hear. Things like 'they love you and can't be without you', 'they have missed you', 'they need you' and so on. They tell you they've changed and promise you it won't be like last time in an attempt to suck you back in to their world. This is called hoovering; where the narcissist will seduce and convince you to return to the abusive relationship you had escaped from. They will do whatever it takes to suck you back in so they can regain power and control you. And with every time you go back it will be worse than the last time but eventually you will understand that the narcissist can never change just as a leopard never changes its spots. Eventually you will stop going back to hell and having a dance with the devil.

Narcissists target empaths

The reason why narcissists attract an empath and vice versa is because the empath is eternally compassionate and ever caring. Always seeing the best in people and wanting to fix and help those who are broken. The empath has a gracious heart and this gracious beautiful heart meets the narcissist's evil heart with its evil desires. As an empath you will see their brokenness and their demons and you yearn to help and rescue them and the narcissists see this about you. They see your beautiful heart and this is why they target you because they know you will have your full attention and focus exclusively on them. In your attempt to love and nurture them they will receive endless narcissistic supply; which is your love, time, energy and care and this will validate and fuel their existence. An empath is a giver and the narcissist is a taker hence the reason why narcissist go after those with empath traits.

They minimize what's important to you

They don't see you, they can't see you; they choose not to see you. They don't see your joy, your sadness, your love, your pain, your success, your accomplishments. They downsize what's important to you and minimize your feelings, thoughts, efforts and accomplishments. They belittle and minimize anything that's important to you in an attempt to ignore and invalidate your experience. Have you ever been so excited about telling them something that's important to you only for them to minimize it and take away its glory? They take away your excitement by making you believe it's nothing special yet if it were to be them then you'd never hear the end of it. The reason narcissists do this is because they can't stand seeing you do better than them or have something they can't have. So they belittle your achievements, steal away your glory because they can't fathom the thought of you being better, doing better or having better.

Narcissists are cynical and pessimistic

Life is hard with a narcissist because they are cynical and pessimistic. They always find a problem to every solution you give them. There's always something wrong and a problem to everything. They love drama and complicating your life will be second nature to them. They work against you and you'll never find them on your side. With a narcissist there is always going to be a problem to everything and it gets better; it's always going to be your problem and your fault somehow. They are downright cynical and negative and will always give you a problem to every solution you give them. They're constantly blaming other people or situations for feeling miserable and even when things go right for them, they find something to complain about.

Here's what they loved about you

Yes this is a hard pill to swallow and the harsh truth you need to bring yourself in acceptance of. The narcissist cannot love you because they are incapable of love. They cannot generate or experience true genuine feelings because they have separated themselves from their truth authentic being. And a false self cannot give you something real such as real love. You may think they did love you at one stage and surely it wasn't all made up in your mind but here's what they loved about you. They loved the way you made them feel, they loved being the centre of your universe, they loved being put on a pedestal for you to uphold and worship. They loved being loved by you and they loved having your time and attention dedicated purely to them. They loved what you were giving them and doing for them because with the narcissist it's always about them and will never be about you.

They make it all about them

Have you ever had a conversation with the narcissist without it turning to be all about them? I doubt it. Narcissists hog any conversation and start talking about how great they are. The conversation may have nothing to do with them yet they can turn it around and make it all about them. They love to constantly talk about their own greatness, achievements and accomplishments; exaggerating everything and making it bigger than what it actually is. They do this to make sure the spot light is on them and it also helps them portray themselves as this confident and self-assured individual. And because they're too busy talking about themselves they will not listen to you and this is why you can never have a conversation with a narcissist because they won't engage in a conversation about you. They're great at making you feel like you don't exist and a conversation with a narcissist will always drain you and make you feel worse than what you did before the conversation. They don't have the time or energy to listen to you yet they'll never shut up talking about themselves. They divert any conversation and make it about them.

They are delusional

Narcissists refuse to deal with reality because they refuse to accept a reality which contradicts what they want to be true. So they would rather live in denial and delude themselves into believing that what is real is actually not real and how they want things to be is real, even though it isn't. Since reality doesn't support their grandiose view of themselves and their life, they choose to live in a fantasy instead. A story they have made themselves and others believe as they would rather live by their own version of the truth than face the truth which goes against everything they've believed in.

They project themselves on you

Narcissists love to project. They project their distorted self on others; their fears and insecurities, their shortcomings and flaws. Whatever demons they have they project them on someone else. They use projection to create a different version of the truth. For example if they say someone else is jealous of them, then you know that the narcissist is the one who is jealous. If they say the other person has treated them poorly then you know they're the one who treated the other person poorly. They project their traits on other people so they don't have to admit their faults or take responsibility for their actions; by always putting the blame and responsibility on someone else. They also do this because they want to show and uphold a perfect image of themselves to the world by putting the fault on the other person; making them look as the 'good guy' in this scenario.

Narcissists are judgmental

Narcissists are so judgmental of everyone else yet very intolerant of anyone judging them. They lash out at the slightest criticism yet they are the first to point out everyone's flaws and shortcomings. They are judgmental and egotistical in ways you cannot comprehend. But you need to remember that narcissists are very insecure and vulnerable and to protect themselves from their vulnerability and weak ego they become judgmental. They shift the focus and attention on the faults of others to distract and protect themselves from their own faults. They don't want to acknowledge and admit they have faults because their weak and fragile self cannot withstand that. They keep themselves busy observing someone else's life and pointing out all their flaws and mistakes than to look at their own wrongdoings; which are many. It's easier for the narcissist to believe there is something wrong with everyone in this world than to admit there is something wrong with them because they cannot possibly sustain a narcissistic injury to their ego.

You can't win a fight with them

Don't fight with a narcissist because it's a battle you'll never win. They feed off conflict; they thrive on drama and chaos, they love division and disagreement. All this grants the narcissist a hit of narcissistic supply, the very thing they can't survive with. They don't care what it's doing to you all they care about is the attention you're giving them to prove their existence and significance in your life. Negative or positive, it doesn't matter to them as long as you are validating their existence and importance in your life. They want you to argue and fight back because in doing so you are exerting power and energy which is the perfect food for their insatiable ego. Then they hoover you after mistreating you only to do it all over again. So the best way to win with a narcissist is by not playing at all, don't engage but disengage.

Inconsiderate towards your feelings

They make you feel guilty for the way you feel and belittle or worse yet mock your pain. They are inconsiderate when it comes to your thoughts and feelings and won't let you express them safely. They will make you believe you're overreacting or just being a little 'too much' so you end up feeling worse than what you did. They invalidate your feelings making you disregard and ignore the way you feel to keep them comfortable. They gaslight you and make you question your own truth and sanity and whether in fact you are overreacting and being a little too much so you begin to ignore the way you feel. Narcissists lack empathy, unwilling to recognise or identity with other people's feelings and needs.

They make promises they can't keep

Narcissists promise you everything but fail to fulfil anything. They make promises they know they won't keep and this is betrayal and manipulation at its best. They start out promising you the world but in the end they're the ones who tear your world apart. They do this to keep you hooked in but sooner or later you will realize that waiting on them is futile and a waste of time. They can't make a promise and keep it, they don't have the decency to keep their word let alone fulfil what they've promised you. You believe them out of the goodness of your heart and give second chances because you want to believe that they're capable of change but to your disappointment they'll always let you down. The narcissist will promise you something and go on about doing the exact opposite to what they've just promised you. They promise you of making your dreams come true but deliver you a nightmare instead. Narcissists make promises they know they won't keep.

They violate your boundaries

Narcissists don't have boundaries so they're not about to respect the boundaries of others. They violate your boundaries and show no respect to your values. They can't take no for an answer because being told no is a form of rejection and narcissists don't take rejection very well. They lack empathy and understanding and struggle to see other people as actual people with thoughts, feelings and emotions so they show little to no respect to other people boundaries. They come with a strong sense of entitlement and self-centeredness so they believe they are above the law and refuse to play by the rules. They violate and break all boundaries because they have no respect or regard to anyone but themselves and they have no issue in disrespecting others for their personal gain and satisfaction.

You can't grow around a narcissist

Being with a narcissist will hinder your growth and how far you can get in life. They are going to be your stumbling block and they are the very thing that is standing between you and all your dreams. You can't grow around the narcissist; they will drag up your past and every mistake you've made and will not allow you to be different. They will remind you of all your shortcomings and flaws to tarnish the way you see yourself making it very hard for you to grow and evolve. You can't heal around the same person who is making you sick and you can't grow around the same person who is determined to stay the same. You will also find that even after you've healed and evolved, the narcissist will still hold on to the old version of you because they cannot fathom the idea of having lost their grip on you.

Exaggerating their achievements and talents

Narcissists have a grandiose sense of self-importance; they exaggerate their achievements and talents. They compensate for their feelings of inferiority by exaggerating and lying about their achievements and talents. You need to know that narcissists don't live in reality, they are living in a fantasy; a reality that does not exist and isn't real. So they have to exaggerate their achievements and talents to make themselves and others believe in their fantasy; a fantasy that makes them feel superior to everyone else. It could be the smallest thing yet they will turn it into an exaggerated achievement and you'll never hear the end of it. The self-flattering statements are often exaggerated, the achievement in itself could be minor but they'll turn it into something major. This is how they puff their sense of self and get a feeling of superiority over everyone else.

The silent treatment

The silent treatment is one of the most commonly used forms of emotional abuse by the narcissist after they've tried everything else and failed. They use the silent treatment to punish their victims for not agreeing with their point of view or their version of the truth. They also use silent treatment to gain power in the relationship and be the one in control. It's also a great way to avoid accountability and taking responsibility for what they did wrong so they avoid speaking to you about it by going silent. And because you are trauma-bonded with them you will have no choice but to go back and make amends, forgiving them for what they did wrong; freeing them from accountability and from facing the consequences of their actions.

They are very insure with very low self-esteem

Don't let their mask of ultra-confidence fool you because behind their mask lies a fragile, insecure, and weak individual. What you see on the outside is not the truth of who they are on the inside. What you see is a false self; a character they are pretending to be to compensate for how they truly feel about themselves. Narcissists are very insecure at their core; they feel undeserving, unworthy, and empty with very low self-esteem. They are vulnerable to the slightest criticism and as a result they set up this false self to protect themselves from having to face their truth. Remember those who pretend to be the strongest are the weakest and those who pretend to be confident are insecure. Eventually their masks fall off and you will see them for who they really are.

They would rather give up than fight

They would rather give up on a relationship and lose someone close to them than to ever admit they're in the wrong, take accountability and attempt to fix their mistakes. Accepting responsibility will make them admit they did something wrong and their ego cannot possibly accept or withstand that. Their ego is so weak and fragile that it can never sustain a narcissistic injury or admit fault even at the expense of losing someone special. They think so highly of themselves and believe they're as close to perfect as anyone could get. So they would rather give up and lose something of value than to actually admit fault and apologize. This is a hard pill to swallow because the narcissist will give up on you way too easily because they would rather lose you than fight for you when all you've been doing is fighting not to lose them.

They will discredit you

When you finally leave the narcissist, you're going to cause immense damage to their ego because they've lost control over you and lost their source of narcissistic supply. That's when they usually begin to discredit you and tell all sorts of lies about you to convince everyone it was all your fault, making people see you in a different light. They intentionally spread deceptive information for the purpose of undermining and discrediting you. This is just another form of their toxic, manipulative tactic to try and get you to engage and suck you back into their world. But whatever you do; do not engage and get back there because the second you're back in their world they've regained power to control and abuse you again. When you make the decision to walk away be sure to stay away knowing the truth will always prevail.

Narcissists don't love themselves

You may think narcissists love themselves but that's not true. They portray like they love themselves but the truth of the matter is they don't love themselves; their 'true' self. They're in love with their false, imaginary self they've created in their mind. They don't love who they truly are hence the reason why they've chosen to abandon their true self and soul to become someone else. Image the level of hatred you have for yourself when you rather be someone else other than who you really are. They love who they think they are not who they actually are and love based on a lie cannot possibly be true. They are incapable of experiencing true love because a false self cannot experience anything true and genuine. They pretend to show the world they are in love with themselves to avoid being seen for the real wounded self; the true self they are constantly running away from.

They are emotionally distant and unavailable

Narcissists are emotionally distant and unavailable so they cannot give you the tender loving care you deserve. They can make themselves available only when they want something but if they're not gaining anything out of it then they will not be considerate and tend to your feelings and needs as a mature, nurturing partner would. You expect them to be there for you when you're down as you would with them but they never are. They'll never be there when you need them because they're not interested in meeting your needs as they are meeting their own. They're either too busy or somehow make it all about themselves completely ignoring how you feel. It's all about them and what they have to gain but when there's nothing it in for them they become distant and unavailable.

Narcissists are pathological liars

Everyone lies and in fact we've all told many lies over time. The narcissist however is a liar; it's not just what they do, it's *who* they are. They are habitual liars. They have the ability to lie to your face effortlessly and be very convincing at it too. They can look you straight in the eye and lie with no problem at all because lying is second nature to them. Think about it the narcissists have lied to themselves, about who they are and they live by their own version of the truth. And how can someone whose entire identity and life is built on lies and deception be ever true to you? You can't find truth in someone who is not real so stop looking for human decency because you're not dealing with a real human. Lying is a powerful way for the narcissist to manipulate and control others and reality. Unlike us, narcissists don't have a conscience so they don't have a moral sense of what's right or wrong so there is nothing to stop them from lying about everything and anything. Narcissists will try and destroy your life with lies to keep you in the dark because their life can be easily destroyed with the truth. They fabricate the truth to protect themselves and they do this by lying to everyone about everything.

Narcissists hold grudges

Narcissists don't forgive instead they hold onto grudges for as long as you can remember and will always remind you of your mistakes even long after the incident had occurred. They cannot forgive so they seek revenge, any way to make you payback for the narcissistic injury you caused their ego. They struggle with forgiving people even for their minor shortcomings and instead seek to avenge themselves in any way, shape or form. They might pretend to have forgiven you but deep down they could be looking for ways to make you pay. Genuine forgiveness is not part of their emotional encompass and this is mainly because the narcissists cannot forgive themselves. And how they treat themselves will be how they treat you.

They come with a sense of entitlement

Narcissists have a sense of entitlement because they see themselves special and above all else so they expect extra care and treatment than anyone else. They are self-centred and selfish people and believe everyone's world should evolve around them so they expect favourable treatment and automatic agreement to their demands. This is why you can never get a narcissist to appreciate what you are doing for them because in their mind this is your duty of care towards them. They feel entitled to everything you have and everything you're doing for them. They expect everyone to comply with their every wish and command. They expect special consideration and treatment because they believe they're extra special, important and superior to all else. The narcissist will never appreciate anything because you can't appreciate something you feel entitled to.

They won't apologize sincerely

You will never get a sincere apology from a narcissist because a sincere apology only comes from self-reflection and admitting what you did was wrong. Good luck trying to get a narcissist to admit fault and take responsibility for what they did. If they do apologize then it's usually for their personal gain; to get you to forgive them and give them another chance to disappoint you with. A sincere apology requires changed behaviour but you will not see a narcissist change the way they behave. So an apology without changed behaviour is another form of abuse and manipulation. They will never admit they're wrong because this will injure their fragile self. So if you're waiting for a narcissist to give you a sincere apology then you could be waiting a long time. Don't put your life on hold any longer waiting for an apology you'll never receive because even if you do it will not be sincere and heartfelt.

They compete with you

There's no such thing as 'us' with a narcissist; it's you against them. It's a battlefield to the narcissist; a competition they are determined to win. Narcissists will compete with you rather than support you and celebrate your accomplishments. They may pretend to be happy for you and admire your accomplishments but deep down they are jealous and will attempt to diminish your accomplishments. Their envy and jealousy arises from their need to be the best and have the best because that's the only way they can maintain their grandiose delusion of self-importance and prestige. They have to downgrade what you've achieved to make you feel small and nothing you do is going to be 'special' or impressive because the smaller they can make you feel, the bigger and better they can feel about themselves.

They're not who you think they are

When you're with a narcissist you get sucked into their fantasy and their own version of reality. They make you believe in the lies about who they are when the truth is completely the opposite of what you're being told. They paint a different picture of who they are to the world so you end up believing this version of them without realizing this is not who they really are. So you fall in love with this version of them, not who they are. Your heart breaks in million pieces when you find out they're not who you thought they were and you've been in love with lie all this time. But sooner or later you need to start seeing them for who they really are, not who you want them to be. You need to stop making excuses for their bad behaviour or deny how they're making you feel. Denying your pain will not make it go away, it'll only grow bigger. And eventually the pain of staying becomes greater than the pain of leaving so you finally decide to walk away and never look back.

They can't handle criticism

They cannot handle criticism because any type of criticism will damage and injure their already fragile ego. Their egos cannot handle it because the ego is weak and highly sensitive when being criticized in any way. They are highly sensitive towards any criticism and a small remark can cause a big reaction yet they are the most insensitive people towards others. They criticize you to demean you and disempower you, evoking insecurity and doubt in you. The narcissists will almost always lash out when criticized or they shut down and punish you through silent treatments because they are highly sensitive to criticism. Their insecure, easily damaged sense of self cannot handle criticism as well as others do.

They sabotage you

Narcissists will not allow you to grow, flourish and succeed in any area of your life because they don't want to see you do better than them. So they sabotage you in all areas of your life especially the areas you're succeeding in. Remember narcissists cannot stand seeing you or others happy because it reminds them of the very thing they can't have. So they attempt to steal away your joy and happiness by creating chaos and drama. They can do this by ruining your mood just before an occasion, or start a fight with you right before a celebration, meeting, holiday; you name it. They will do whatever it takes to prevent you from flourishing and succeeding in your life by sabotaging you because your level of happiness and success threatens to take away their power over you.

Narcissists are unfaithful

Seeing as lying comes easily to the narcissists so does infidelity and betrayal. The word loyalty does not exist in their dictionary because they don't feel like normal rules should be applied to them. They are skilled at cheating and covering up because they are skilled liars and manipulators. This is who they are and they believe they can get away with anything. Narcissists don't like to be limited to one source of supply but in fact they like to have a couple or at least one another because this gives them enhanced power and control. They are constantly on the lookout trying to fill their narcissistic supply and what better way to do this than to engage in a number of affairs and relationships. They see themselves as 'above the law' so they don't feel like playing by the rules because this will take away their sense of superiority and make them like everyone else.

They abandon you

Narcissists will abandon you when you're in need of them the most even when you've been there for them all the time. They cannot possibly look after you as a normal loving figure would because they are inherently selfish and their only concern is their needs and wants. They abandon you in times of difficulty, hardship or illness and show you no empathy when you're suffering or going through a difficult time. They have no concern to your wellbeing and needs because they only care about themselves and what you have to give them. So if you're counting on the narcissist to be there for you when you need them the most, then think again because that's when they usually abandon you and will not look after you the way you've looked after them.

Narcissists are tight with money

Narcissists are cheap when it comes to money and they would rather not spend anything than spend a dime. For a narcissist money is a source of power and status. They want to have money so they can show people their perfect, 'rich' life to get a sense of superiority and status. They will do what it takes to take control of money because with money comes attention, status, and power; all the things a narcissist yearns for. They have no problem in using your money, time and resources but they are stingy with theirs. They have no problem depending on you for everything because they would rather access all of your resources and reserve theirs.

They intentionally withhold their attention

Narcissists withhold the very things they know you need to control and manipulate you in giving them what they need instead. They withhold affection and appreciation to keep their victims enslaved to their toxic cycle of abuse. When they withdraw and withhold their attention, you begin to chase and beg them and this gives them exactly what they need; your energy, time and attention; the perfect narcissistic supply. You begin attempting to please them and do whatever it takes to regain the love and appreciation you once had at the beginning of the relationship and this is how they manipulate you into giving them what they need instead. You will always have to fight, chase and beg for their love, time and affection and in doing so you are giving the narcissist exactly what they need so it's a win-lose situation; a win for them, a loss for you.

They micromanage your life

In order for the narcissist to establish control over all aspects of your life, they begin to micromanage your life in the name of 'love'. They pretend to be the caring, protective, loving type disguising their manipulative tactics as a form of love. So they begin to control who you interact with, where you go, what you do, how you speak and how you behave. They will begin making demands that will take up most of your time in an attempt to stop you from doing anything for yourself or anyone else. Narcissists have the need to control everyone and everything around to them to maintain their version of reality and self.

They treat you with contempt

You need to understand that the narcissists are not who they claim to be; this super confident individual with very high self-esteem. On the contrary narcissists are the most insecure people you will ever meet; they come with a very fragile and damaged self-esteem. So treating you with contempt comes from their level of insecurity because they need to put you down for them to feel superior. They don't like seeing other people succeed or be happy in their lives because they cannot possibly withstand the idea of someone else being better than them or surpassing them in any way. So they begin to humiliate, shame and tear down anyone they feel threated by; treating you with contempt and superiority to make you believe you are below them.

Narcissists love triangulation

The narcissist will always bring a third party into the mix to enhance their feeling of superiority, boost up their fragile self-esteem and gain power and control over other people. This is called triangulation; when the narcissist brings in a third person in an attempt to divide and conquer their victims. It is all one big game to the narcissist; to gain power and control giving them a feeling of importance and high regard. They triangulate people to create discord, jealousy and confusion and they enjoy the attention given to them as a result of this triangulation. Narcissists are very selfish and highly illogical; they enjoy any attention given to them and don't care if it's positive or negative. The attention is validating their existence and importance in your life and the other person's life and this is all they care about. They triangulate you with other people to make you question your worthiness and to push you to compete for their attention.

They'll be there when things are great

They'll be there when things are great and if not then they're nowhere to be found. They'll be there when you're doing well and feeling well but never there when you need their support. The narcissist will be present and accommodating when you have everything going for you but that's only because they want to see what's in it for them. Remember with the narcissists it's always about what they can gain from you. They leech off your wellbeing, success and resources. They don't want to work hard so they prefer piggybacking someone else's hard work and effort than having to work for it themselves. But when you need them for something or just need a listening ear or a shoulder to cry on, they won't be found.

Masters of instilling doubts

They are the masters of making you believe in lies and instilling seeds of doubts into your mind about yourself, others and life. They sow seeds of doubts to undermine your reality by denying facts, replacing the truth with their lies. This is called gaslighting in narcissism where the narcissist sows seeds of doubt in your mind to make you question your truth, sanity, memory or judgement. This is a form of emotional abuse where they force you to question your reality; your own thoughts, events and memories to the point where you think you're losing your mind. Gaslighting is a tactic they use to tear you down and erode your identity in order to gain power and control over you. They brainwash you and this is how you lose your sense of identity and self-worth because you have believed in their version of who you are and forgotten who you truly are.

You can't fix a narcissist

We fall into the trap of thinking we can fix them if we just stayed a little longer and tried a little harder. But what you don't realize at the time is that you are breaking yourself in the attempt of fixing them. You can't fix them or change them because you can't change someone who doesn't see an issue in their actions. Narcissists are delusional and self-deceived individuals and they believe they are the centre of the universe and you can't change a person like that. Change requires self-reflection and humility in admitting one's flaws and shortcoming and a genuine interest in changing oneself. Narcissists are very resistant to change and they live in a fantasy which tells them everyone else is at fault; releasing them from the need to change. Self-reflection damages their perfect image of self and they will not allow their assumption of their own perfection to be challenged. You have to accept the fact that you can't change them and it's not your responsibility to rescue them. Your responsibility is to rescue yourself from this living hell and set yourself free.

Narcissists can't handle rejection

Narcissists don't handle rejection very well, in fact, they can't. When a narcissist is rejected or denied something they want, it injures their already fragile and weak ego and self-esteem. Whilst rejection hurts us all, we process the pain of rejection in different ways than narcissists do. When narcissists experience rejection they go on a blind rage behaving in a poisonous and destructive way. Rejecting or denying the narcissist will result in conflict, rage and abusive behaviour to sabotage and damage you emotionally because you have just challenged their confidence and sense of self. Rejection causes a major narcissistic injury to the narcissist resulting in a dangerous and harmful rage.

They don't play by the rules

To the narcissist it's all about winning at any cost because winning to them is above playing fair. They don't like to play by the rules because this makes them like everybody else. They feel like they are above the rules and laws so they simply don't care about what's right or wrong. A relationship with a narcissist is one big game to them; it isn't about love, consideration or fairness but it's about them having the upper hand and winning at all cost by getting what they want. They only care about themselves and their needs and will do what it takes to have those needs met even if it meant at the expense of damaging another soul. To them it's one big game; a game you can never win because they have no obligation to play fairly by the rules and they bend and change them whenever they see fit.

Their charm wears off

Narcissists truly believe that every soul on this planet adores them and hold them in high regard. And they assume those who don't are just jealous of them. They have the ability to make a great first impression so they can be very charming and convincing at first winning people's approval and admiration. Their charming personality obtains praise and favor from people they first meet but sooner or later their charm wears out because it was never real to begin with. With time their selfish personality and destructive behaviour causes people to see the real them and run as far away from them as they can.

Being with a narcissist is exhausting

Being with a narcissist is exhausting and daunting at the same time because it is and will always be a one-sided relationship. A relationship that will always drain you and never pour into you and this is why you feel so tired, drained and discouraged most of the time. The narcissist comes with an insatiable ego so they will always want more and ask for more. They want more love, attention, fame, status, money, you name it, and nothing will ever be enough. They make demands that are impossible for you to meet and maintain over time. You'll constantly be walking on eggshells and will be in a permanent fight-or-flight mode. This is what an abusive relationship does to you; no matter what you do or how much you give, you will never be able to satisfy the narcissist and this will bring you to complete exhaustion; of mind, body and spirit.

They idolize and depreciate

You will find that the narcissists will idolize and depreciate people depending on what they can get from them. They will idolize those people who make them feel good about themselves and depreciate those who don't. They love being the centre of attention and they will idolize those people whose gaze is fixated exclusively on them. Narcissists look at others to see what they can gain from them and they will remain with you for as long as you are giving them their narcissistic supply. But this cannot last forever and when the narcissist has already extracted all the supply they can get from you they will start to depreciate you. They depreciate people when they see no further benefit or gain and this is when they usually discard and replace you with new supply. But don't take it personal because they will do to everyone as they did to you. Narcissists don't grow and evolve; they remain the same and repeat.

They appear to be independent

Narcissists put on a front; a façade so what you see on the outside is not what you see on the inside. Even salt looks like sugar but they're very different. On the surface they appear to be very independent and undisturbed. They appear to be so confident and secure you start to wonder why you can't feel the same about yourself. But you always need to go back to the one powerful truth; narcissists have put on a false self so they are not real. So even though they may appear to be extremely independent and self-sufficient you need to know this isn't how they truly feel on the inside. On the contrary they are very dependent; depending on everyone else for their narcissistic supply because without it they cannot exist.

They disguise their insults as jokes

Narcissists disguise their insults, teasing or mocking remarks as jokes. They may say something to you as a 'joke' but there is usually an undercurrent beneath their remarks. This is how they gaslight you and get the better of you. They insult you and make remarks to make you question yourself and if in fact what they're saying about you happens to be the truth. They say things like 'you're just crazy', 'why you're being weird', 'you're just jealous' as a joke when in fact they are instilling seeds of doubts about how you see yourself so you can believe in their version of the truth. And if you happen to pull them up on it they get away by saying it was a joke and you need to chill a little. This subtle blame shifting will make you feel bad for the way you acted and you go on apologizing for something you didn't do wrong.

There is nothing wrong with you

Once you receive the revelation that the narcissist is someone who is not real you will no longer believe in their lies about you. When you know they are not a true self then you will also know that nothing they say is true either. They want to control and manipulate you so you can believe in their version of the truth rather than find out the truth about who they are. You see once you know the truth; the truth will set you free and when you know the narcissist is a pathological liar who habitually lies about everything then it becomes easier not to believe in anything they say. Why believe in what a liar has to say when all they say is a lie?

Take the lead or be led

If you're going to wait for the narcissist to change or apologize for all the chaos they've brought into your life then you will be waiting a very long time. You're waiting for something that is not going to happen. Don't wait on the narcissist for anything because when you wait on them you have in fact given them power over you and your life. And rest assured the narcissists will always lead you astray because they are blind themselves without any direction or purpose. But instead take back your power and take charge of your life; take the lead and become the leader of your own life. Start giving yourself what you want the narcissist to give you. Are you after love, kindness and understanding? Then start by giving yourself what you're waiting on the narcissist to give you. The narcissist cannot give you what you need but you certainly can. Take the lead or be led; the choice is yours.

The narcissist can't heal you

I know how much you want the person who's hurt you to be the one to heal you but that's not going to happen. You may not have had a say in your pain but you do have a say in your healing and the healer you are looking for is yourself. Healing ourselves is our responsibility and the more we look to the narcissist for our healing the more we delay the process. The devastating destruction the narcissist brings into your life is heartbreaking and soul-crushing but don't let the pain make you give up on yourself. Don't prolong your healing journey; take your focus off the narcissist and put in on your healing. The narcissist may have broken you down but take this as an opportunity to rebuild something more beautiful. You are the healer you have been looking for because you hold the power to change yourself from within.

Don't feel sorry for them

The narcissists are experts at playing the victim and they do a good job playing the role. But whatever you do, don't feel sorry for them because the second you do is the second they've regained power over you. Pity and compassion are two different emotions which will put you in two different states of mind. You can be compassionate towards them but don't pity them because pity will make you join them in their misery and you will absorb their dense, negative feelings. This is how narcissists crawl back in your life and get you to give them what they need. The play the victim role and you believe them so you take them back and forgive them for their actions without any consequences. This is just another form of manipulation so whatever you do don't feel sorry for them because they show no genuine remorse.

Do not engage with the narcissist

Do not engage but always disengage. Now don't worry I already know how easier said than done this is but you must learn how to do this especially if you can't get away from the narcissist and go no contact. Narcissists thrive on drama; they feed off negativity and live in chaos and disorder. They know how to push your buttons and trigger you into giving them a reaction. The say or do things purposely to upset you and get you going because they want you to take the bait and fight back. When you engage with the narcissist you have just lost the game because playing with a toxic person is a game you will never win. On the contrary engaging with the narcissist will make you lose something so valuable; your peace. Remember you are not dealing with a normal human being who is capable of seeing sense and being considerate towards others. You are dealing with a narcissist who is self-centred and selfish and will do what it takes to gain their narcissistic supply. Disengage and you will stop their food supply and when you stop feeding something it will starve to death. This is when the narcissist normally falls off your experience or stops harassing you because you are not giving them what they need.

You were in love with an illusion

You were in love with an illusion, a person who doesn't exist. You fell in love with the person you thought they were or the person you wanted them to be but in both cases that's not who they are. Narcissists are extremely charming when you first meet them because you see this confident, self-sufficient, secure person who is telling you all the right things and doing all the right things. Not knowing this is just a façade to cover up who they really are and how they feel about themselves. So you fall in love with this version of them, a version built on an illusion, but in time their mask starts to come off and you begin to see a person you no longer recognise. You begin wondering why they've changed so drastically and you start to work harder in an attempt to get the old them back. But what you don't realise is that they didn't change; the mask just came off and this is who they really are, who they have always been. So you have been in love with who you thought they were not who they really are.

It's normal if you miss them

Just because you know who they are now doesn't stop you from missing them. You will miss them especially if you've been involved with them romantically. Missing them is normal because you loved them and it was real to you. They were a big part of your life and you will miss that part of your life and wish for things to go back to the way they were. But the narcissists are not real so your relationship with them wasn't real in the sense that it was built on a false foundation and anything false cannot withstand the test of time. Only that which is true and real withstands and endures and your relationship with the narcissist wasn't because you were with someone who is not real. But it's completely normal to miss them and don't beat yourself for feeling this way because your feelings are real and valid. Here's the thing though; missing them doesn't mean you need them back in your life. You can still miss them and not want them back because you know they are no good to your heart and soul. So it's okay to miss them by just because you miss them it doesn't mean you need to be with them.

Stay off social media and delete everything

Once you break ties with the narcissist you need to stay off social media for a little while and delete everything that would remind you of them and trigger you back to painful memories. It's a human tendency to check their social media and see what they are up to, who they're with and so on. But this isn't going to benefit you in any way, on the contrary this will always trigger you back to painful memories and you will relive the experience all over again. You also need to delete everything that reminds you of them; photos, text messages, emails, number and everything that ties you to them in any way. When you leave a narcissist you begin purging of the soul and to do this you need to purge your life also of anything to do with them. It's about cleansing your environment and surrounding as well and you do this by deleting everything and breaking all ties to them. This is really difficult to do because this is all you have left of them and your time with them but you need to make your healing a priority and remove any stumbling block out of your way. And anything that reminds you of the narcissist will be a stumbling block to you so be sure to remove them out of your way and focus on your healing.

Give up the fight

Give up the fight with the narcissist. Give up the struggle, the turmoil, the confusion, the destruction. Give it all up. You can't fix everything and you certainly can't fix or save the narcissist. It's not your responsibility and even if you tried you will end up breaking yourself instead. The narcissists don't want to try, they don't want to put in any effort; they simply don't care. Being with a narcissist will have you be in a constant fight-or-flight mode; you'll always find yourself fighting against everyone and everything seems to be hard work. Nothing flows effortlessly and everything feels like a struggle. Narcissists don't want to make peace; they are not interested in compromising or meeting you half way so you need to give up the fight because it's a battle you'll never win. They will always come up with issues and excuses making your life a lot harder and stressful than it really is. They will always find a way to kill, steal and destroy. Relationships are worth fighting for yes but not when you're the only one fighting for a one-sided relationship.

Don't equate your self-worth with the narcissist

Don't equate your self-worth and value with what the narcissist is or isn't doing. If you're going to look at the narcissist for validation and approval you'll always set yourself up for failure and disappointment. The narcissists do not approve of anyone because they don't approve of themselves. It's easy to be discouraged and disheartened when they don't see you, appreciate you or acknowledge you. But don't let their actions stop you from seeing your own self-worth. It's not about the narcissists being able to recognise and acknowledge your worth; it's about you recognising your own self-worth. It's about how you see yourself. The narcissist will always let you down one way or another and if you continue looking at the narcissist to value you then you'll always be selling yourself short. Don't let someone who doesn't know your value tell you how much you're worth.

You need to forgive them

Unless you truly forgive the narcissist in your life then you cannot begin again. Unforgiveness will only hinder you; your healing and your growth. You might think it's going to affect the narcissist but it will only affect you and make things worse for you. Unforgiveness keeps you stuck in a place you don't want to be in. The bitterness and resentment you harbor in your heart will hurt you more. It's important to understand that forgiveness is not excusing their behaviour or the pain they've inflicted on you but it is about setting yourself free from that pain. When you forgive you set yourself free from them and what they did to you and you take back your power. They may have hurt you beyond words but don't hurt yourself more by holding onto the pain longer than you need to. Letting go is a process but make sure you are making progress in the process to let go of what is hurting your heart and soul. Forgiveness is not about the narcissist; it's about setting yourself free because you deserve peace and freedom.

Don't go back to the narcissist

It takes a great amount of power and grace to break free from the narcissist because they have a powerful spiritual hold over you. Leaving the narcissist will cost you your old self and old life and you will walk away from them never being the same again. They turn your world upside down and tear your heart apart giving you an opportunity to go from within and heal yourself once and for all. This will be the hardest thing you do but also the best thing you can do for yourself and then you will realise the worst thing that happened to you has also been the best thing that could've happened to you. And when you get back on your feet don't go running back to the same person who broke you down. Don't go back to the narcissist because it will always be the same devastating experience. Don't go back to someone you needed the power and the grace of God to break you free from. When you get back up on your feet be sure to move forward with your life and not backward because what you want is ahead of you not behind you.

You need to let go

You need to let the narcissist go and letting go of someone you love is going to be hardest thing you do. But there comes a time where you need to let go of the narcissist and all that's happened with them. Letting go is hard and painful but staying with the narcissist will be harder and more painful. When the pain of staying becomes greater than the pain of letting go then you know it's time for you to begin letting go. I know how hard it is to accept that the life you had envisioned with this person will no longer be; when all your wishes and dreams have been shattered. It's devastating and heartbreaking to say the least but the only way to move on is by letting go of how you wanted your life to be. Your life with the narcissist was never meant to work out; it was always about awakening you into who you really are. And just because life didn't turn out the way you wanted it to doesn't mean it won't turn out far better and more beautiful than the life you had envisioned. Let go of the life you wanted so you can receive the life you deserve.

No contact is a must

In order to break free from the narcissist you need to go on a strict no contact rule. This is hard if the narcissist is a family member or kids are involved, in this case limited contact will suffice. But if you were romantically linked with the narcissist and there are no ties that hold you to them then going no contact is a must. This is going to be extremely difficult because by this time you are addicted to the narcissist as an addict addicted to drugs and going no contact is going to be excruciatingly painful because you are detoxing and cleansing your soul from all that poison. The narcissist has poisoned your soul and you need to purge yourself of all that poison and toxicity and the only way you can begin to do this is by going no contact and having nothing to do with the narcissist. You can't heal a wound if you keep touching it so in order for you to begin healing you need to close the door to your source of pain; the narcissist.

Forgive yourself

Yes you need to forgive the narcissist and everything you've been through but you also need to forgive the most important person here; yourself. We tend to be hard on ourselves and we hold ourselves accountable for every mistake we make but making mistakes is part of learning. We all make mistakes and this is how we're going to learn. Don't be hard on yourself by saying I wish I knew then what I know now. Forgive yourself for not knowing what you didn't know before you lived through it. Going through the experience was what taught you what you know now so everything you have been through is helping you become the best version of yourself. Accept that you are not perfect and you're allowed to make mistakes and learn from them because we are all here learning and growing. Forgive yourself for not knowing you were with a narcissist because rarely anyone does before they experience it. Be kind and gentle with yourself and it's only when you forgive yourself you can begin again. You can be your worst enemy or become your very own best friend; the choice is yours

You gave it your absolute best

You will start to question if you could have done better or said better and maybe it might've worked out with the narcissist after all. But let me remind you that your life with the narcissist was never meant to work out. And let me also remind you that you gave it your absolute best. You were the one trying to make it work, you were the one who gave and continued giving without getting anything in return. So you gave it your absolute best and don't sit there thinking about what could've been, if it should've been it would've been. But the narcissist in your life was only there to help you shed your layers so you can return to your true authentic self. Nothing you could've said or done would've changed the outcome because the narcissist had no intention of building a genuine, long-lasting relationship with you. So don't look back and wish for things to be different. At one point you will need to turn the page because you can't start the next chapter of your life if you're busy rereading your last one.

You will come out of this stronger

You're familiar with the saying what doesn't kill you makes you stronger right? It certainly will because nothing has the power to kill or destroy you. The narcissist may have broken your heart and soul but they cannot break your spirit and the storm you're in now will in fact make you stronger. The narcissist will tear you down but this so you could build yourself back up into a stronger and wiser version of yourself. There will be moments that will rip your heart out and tear it into million pieces and you will never be the same person again. And that's okay because your new self will cost you your old self and these moments will make you stronger, wiser and kinder. Cry and scream if you need to but eventually you will need to get back up, straighten that crown of yours and keep it moving forward because you will come out of this stronger. You had to travel to the lowest lows to get to the highest highs.

You deserve better

When you are involved with a narcissist you begin to lose yourself and forget who you are. Somewhere along the line you lost yourself and you don't remember your worth anymore. They erode your identity and cloud your vision so you forget your self-worth and value and forgetting the one simple yet very powerful truth; you deserve better! You deserve better than this because you are worthy of God's best but we start out not knowing our worth so we settle for just about anything. But sooner or later you need to realise that you deserve better. Stop wasting your time and energy chasing after people or making things right with the wrong one. There comes a time where you need to be willing to lose it all to gain it all and you can only do this when you realise you deserve better. Don't let people stay in your life longer than they deserve and you need to walk away from what you want to get what you deserve.

A bigger purpose

There is a bigger purpose to why the narcissists came into your life. It wasn't an accident or a mistake but it was for a purpose; a big purpose. The narcissist was presented in your life to awaken you spiritually and bring your subconscious fears, beliefs and demons into light so you can now see them, face them, and overcome them. The devastating destruction a narcissist brings into your life is designed to tear down the false you; your outer shell so that the new, *real* you can emerge. The narcissist brings all your fears, traumas, and pain to light; they echo in resonance that which already existed within you from the beginning of time granting you an enormous opportunity to finally heal yourself back to wholeness and unity. Narcissistic abuse will push you to embark the inner journey of learning how to love and heal yourself and you might not have gotten to that level of healing if the narcissist hadn't been presented in your life. It is an inner journey leading you back *home* to yourself.

You are not alone in this

You are not alone in all this. You are not alone in this mess, chaos and what seems to be a horrible nightmare. Many people, in fact, a lot of people have been through what you're going through right now so we are all in this together. It might seem like you are on your own; alone in a very dark place desperately waiting to see the light at the end of the tunnel but I am here to reassure you that you are not alone. I am here to assure you that you will see the light but not at the end of the tunnel; *you* will become the light in the tunnel and light your way forward. You will become the light you have been desperately waiting for and you will become the person you needed everyone to be for you. You will heal, you will grow and you will thrive after your narcissistic abuse given that you take your focus off anything that may distract or hinder your healing. What seems like the worst thing to happen to you will turn out to be the best thing that could've happened for you. The darkness you're in today will lead you into the light and your biggest lessons will turn into your greatest blessings. You are not alone. You can do this. I believe in you, God believes in you, we all believe in you.

Will *you* believe in yourself?

"To be reborn, you have to die first."

Lucien Carr

"So do not fear, for I am with you; do not be dismayed, for I am your God. I will strengthen you and help you; I will uphold you with my righteous right hand."

Isaiah 41:10

About the Author

Noor Niami is an author, spiritual mentor and motivational speaker but above all she is a woman of God and a believer. Christ alone defines the woman she is and her identity is built purely on Him. Her passion to help others has become her purpose in life and she is determined to empower those who have been hurt and heal the broken-hearted by sharing her personal journey and experiences. Coming from a place of brokenness herself she knows what it feels like to be in that dark place desperately waiting to see the light at the end of the tunnel. It wasn't until she refused to wait any longer and decided to become the light she needed instead. And from there on her mission to empower people around the world began. She is determined be a living testimony to God's unfailing love, grace, and mercy. And she wants to assure you that the pain you've been feeling now can't compare to the joy that is coming.

For more information visit:
www.noorniami.com

Narcissists 101

CPSIA information can be obtained
at www.ICGtesting.com
Printed in the USA
BVHW070929281221
625045BV00009B/269